Lincoln Christian College

# *Evangelicals in Search of Identity*

# Evangelicals in Search of Identity

CARL F. H. HENRY
Th.D., Ph.D.

WORD BOOKS, Publisher
Waco, Texas

ISBN 0–87680–461–X
Library of Congress catalog card number: 76–2856
Printed in the United States of America

Carl F. H. Henry
Publications by Word Books

*The God Who Shows Himself (1966)
*Evangelicals at the Brink of Crisis (1967)

By Other Publishers

*A Doorway to Heaven (1941)
*Successful Church Publicity (1942)
*The Uneasy Conscience of Modern Fundamentalism (1947)
  Remaking the Modern Mind (1948)
*Giving a Reason for Our Hope (1949)
*The Protestant Dilemma (1949)
*Notes on the Doctrine of God (1949)
*Fifty Years of Protestant Theology (1950)
*The Drift of Western Thought (1951)
*Personal Idealism and Strong's Theology (1951)
*Glimpses of a Sacred Land (1953)
*Christian Personal Ethics (1957)
*Evangelical Responsibility in Contemporary Theology (1957)
  Aspects of Christian Social Ethics (1964)
*Frontiers in Modern Theology (1966)
*Faith at the Frontiers (1969)
  A Plea for Evangelical Demonstration (1971)
*New Strides of Faith (1972)

Symposiums

  Contemporary Evangelical Thought (1957)
  Revelation and the Bible (1959)

*Out of print        56357

*The Biblical Expositor*, 3 vols. (1960)
*Basic Christian Doctrines* (1962)
*Christian Faith and Modern Theology* (1964)
*Jesus of Nazareth: Saviour and Lord* (1966)
*Fundamentals of the Faith* (1969)

*Baker's Dictionary of Christian Ethics* (1973)

# Contents

Editor's Preface  *9*

Foreword  *11*

1. A Wavering Evangelical Initiative  *19*

2. Heritage from the Past  *25*

3. Decade of Gains and Losses  *33*

4. Signs of Evangelical Disunity  *41*

5. Conflict over Biblical Inerrancy  *48*

6. Strife over Social Concerns  *57*

7. Reaction and Realignment  *65*

8. Toward a Brighter Day  *73*

9. Moving on Media Frontiers  *81*

10. Vision of a Uniting Task  *89*

# Editor's Preface

Dr. Carl F. H. Henry's *The Uneasy Conscience of Modern Fundamentalism* (1947) was a potent 75-page tract that prodded American evangelicals to rethink their reactionary social withdrawal and to renew their influence in the public realm. Ten years later the Christian Reformed scholar Dirk Jellema wrote that "the 'manifesto' of neo-evangelicalism, if one single thrust had to be picked, would probably be Henry's *The Uneasy Conscience of Modern Fundamentalism*, which really amounts to an ardent plea for a neo-evangelical ethics" (in *Contemporary Evangelical Thought*, New York, Channel Press, 1957, p. 130). In the intervening years Dr. Henry's literary contributions have in certain major respects paced recent evangelical theological and ethical thought. Seminary professor on some of the nation's most prestigious evangelical campuses, author of more than twenty books (some have been translated into Korean, Norwegian, and Spanish), editor of numerous significant symposium efforts, he also served as editor of *Christianity Today* during its first twelve years. Louis Cassels, late religion editor of United Press International, singled him out as "probably the most noted evangelical theologian in the United States." As lecturer-at-large for World Vision International, his teaching and lecture ministry has been worldwide.

Widely credited as a leading evangelical opinion-maker and frequently quoted by the national press and newsmagazines, he has influenced evangelical theological perspective much as Billy Graham has penetrated evangelistic frontiers. What Dr. Henry says here about the present crossroads crisis of the evangelical movement rises from a lifetime of vigorous concern for the Christian cause in the modern world. This present tract, *Evangelicals in Search of Identity*, like *Uneasy Conscience* in the last generation, speaks to a new era of evangelical peril and offers some mature and provocative observations.

# *Foreword*

SOME READERS MAY CONSIDER THESE ABRASIVE
vignettes an act of God. Others may ascribe them
to a quite different genealogy. Still others, however, may find them too congenial to label them
an affront.

My intention, believe me, is not simply to rub
some fellow evangelicals the wrong way. Nor, on
the other hand, is it merely to provide a relaxing
massage. My purpose is to delineate from the en-

during resources shared by evangelical Christians some of those dynamic vitalities without which we will register less and less impact on the public scene and in the life of our generation.

Much like *The Uneasy Conscience of Modern Fundamentalism* (1947), the following chapters developed as a series intended for magazine publication, but were given book form unexpectedly through the spontaneous suggestion of a publisher. It was William B. Eerdmans, Sr., who almost thirty years ago felt that a little book would more effectively jolt fundamentalist conscience than would a series of monthly jeremiads; subsequent events proved him right.

Last October, at the season's colorful best, I drove to North Carolina to deliver some Staley Distinguished Christian Scholar Lectures. Along the way I chatted with Mrs. Henry about the growing "green edges" of the evangelical movement. Speaking at once of approaching springtime and promised harvest, yet also of a certain immaturity that leaves the outcome in doubt, the modifier "green" is doubly appropriate. We talked among other things about the remarkable exuberance (and perhaps even occasional rashness) of the young evangelicals and the reactionary stance of some elder statesmen (who may seem to some observers to be overstaying their influence). We commented on the notable opportunities opening to evangelical Christianity because of the collapse of ecumenism and the internal confusion of theologically pluralistic denominations, while at the same time a revival of past controversies and projection of new differences augured a very real prospect for evangelical fragmentation.

In recent months an abundance of mail has come from evangelicals on virtually all margins of these concerns—young scholars and young activists, pastors and professors, writers who have long shared in the witness of *Christianity Today*, and a number of senior statesmen as well. Much of this correspondence conveys a spirit of apprehension over current evangelical commitments and strategy, and also disappointment over the seeming deflection that has detoured evangelical opportunities. Something untoward seems to have happened on the way to the movement's brightest prospects.

Making the most of an unpreempted half-day before my lectures began, I decided to write on these issues for Footnotes in *Christianity Today*. But my scribblings soon outran the stipulated word limits. By the time we were homeward bound to Virginia I had completed a second segment, but found that I would need even more space to unburden a troubled spirit. During the following week the initial articles quickly multiplied into a series of six; during a flight to a dialogue on a seminary campus I added a seventh.

In St. Louis I was having breakfast with Floyd Thatcher, vice president and executive editor of Word Books, which will soon publish my four-volume theological tome on *God, Revelation and Authority* (the first two will appear about Thanksgiving 1976). We were discussing the turbulence in religious circles today when I mentioned the projected magazine series *Evangelicals in Search of Identity*. Mr. Thatcher suggested that the comments appear, as had *Uneasy Conscience*, in the form of a small book. Thus what had become a series of ten essays scheduled in *Christianity Today* now appears also as a unit.

The evangelical movement has as its distinctive heritage the scriptural Word of God and the regenerating gospel of Jesus Christ. Through the 1966 World Congress on Evangelism a special worldwide momentum was imparted to the movement. In *Evangelicals at the Brink of Crisis*, written immediately after that Congress and published early in 1967, I expressed the personal conviction that "the next ten years—the decade between now and the end of 1975—are critical ones for both conciliar ecumenism and evangelical Christianity. If conciliar ecumenism continues to repress the evangelical witness, and prevents it from coming to formative ecumenical influence, then conciliar ecumenism can only bog into a retarded form of Christianity." I think the adverse fortunes of conciliar ecumenism in the last decade supply an eloquent commentary on this warning; from the plight of once-prestigious Union Theological Seminary in New York to the waning influence of the National Council of Churches and the failing health of the pluralistic churches, one sees a picture of evident decline.

But my observation did not stop there. "And," I continued, "if evangelical Christians do not join heart to heart, will to will and mind to mind across their multitudinous fences, and do not deepen their loyalties to the Risen Lord of the Church, they may well become—by the year 2000—a wilderness cult in a secular society with no more public significance than the ancient Essenes in their Dead Sea caves."

This present series of Footnotes emerged because I think that both the Watergate era without and mounting evangelical dissension within suggest that we are farther along the bleak road to those lonely caves than many evangelicals realize.

I offer these chapters with the prayer that we who will one day stand together in Christ's presence may yet find and support each other here in these days of tragic human need to identify and implement evangelical duties and incalculable opportunities.

*Carl F. H. Henry*

*Arlington, Virginia*
*New Year's Eve, 1975/76*

# 1.
# *A Wavering Evangelical Initiative*

TWENTY-FIVE YEARS AGO THERE WERE SIGNS that the long-caged lion would break its chains and roar upon the American scene with unsuspected power. The evangelical movement's mounting vitality baffled a secular press, beguiled by ecumenical spokesmen for liberal pluralism into regarding conservative Christianity as a fossil-cult destined to early extinction.

While modernist disbelief and neoorthodox universalism scotched the indispensability of conversion, the Graham evangelistic crusades demonstrated anew the gospel's regenerating power.

Fuller Theological Seminary in 1947 brought a higher dimension to most evangelical divinity learning. The Evangelical Theological Society at midcentury canopied hundreds of scholars commited to scriptural inerrancy and hoped to shape a theological renaissance. Evangelical books of philosophical and theological power were on the increase: G. C. Berkouwer, J. Oliver Buswell, Gordon Clark, Cornelius Van Til, E. J. Carnell, Bernard Ramm and others paced the way as J. Gresham Machen had done a half-century earlier. Vigorous symposium and commentary series appeared. The National Association of Evangelicals, founded in 1942, rallied a service constituency of 10 million American evangelicals. *Christianity Today* united scattered evangelical contributors from all denominations in a common theological, evangelistic and social witness. Garnering an impressive paid circulation of 175,000, the magazine enlisted the loyalties of many disenchanted with fundamentalist far right and liberal left; scholars like D. Elton Trueblood now aggressively championed evangelical rational theism.

Aiming to penetrate the secular intellectual arena with young educators holding an informed Christian life and world view, leaders met and talked of a Christian University. This vision, attenuated through many delays, issued finally in a mobile fellowship of scholars, the Institute for Advanced Christian Studies. Meanwhile the Consortium of Christian Colleges emerged to link evangelical campuses in new cooperative effort.

In a time when ecumenical missionary enthusiasm was beginning to wane, the five missionaries martyred by Auca Indians underscored evangelical Christianity's frontier evangelistic concern. Evangelistically committed churches were expanding; some "third force" churches registered post-war growth rates exceeding 500 percent. The World Congress on Evangelism, sponsored in 1966 by *Christianity Today*, gathered evangelists from all continents for an accelerated world thrust.

Church historian Sydney Ahlstrom writes of this "rapidly growing force in American Christianity" in terms of a "vast, inchoate multitude of earnest Christians and a much more dynamic and exclusivistic 'third force' " (*A Religious History of the American People*, Harper & Row, 1966, p. 959).

While he is still on the loose, and still sounding his roar, the evangelical lion is nonetheless slowly succumbing to an identity crisis. The noteworthy cohesion that American evangelicals gained in the sixties has been fading in the seventies through multiplied internal disagreements and emerging counterforces.

The world fundamentalist conference scheduled June 15–22, 1976, in Edinburgh, Scotland, indicates that despite the weakened influence of Carl McIntire, the evangelical far right is regathering for a massive initiative all its own.

In its post-Lausanne Congress (1974) para-ecumenical thrust, the World Evangelical Fellowship wavers between those who want sole emphasis on cooperative evangelism and those who insist that the gospel's social implications are not optional. The so-called American "evangelical establishment"—represented prominently by the National Association of Evangelicals (its impact curtailed by strategy and money limitations), the Billy Graham Evangelistic Association, many evangelical college and seminary administrators, and more recently also by Campus Crusade for Christ—so elevates personal evangelism above other concerns that the Christian faith's sociocultural interests hold seemingly marginal focus. That courageous minority of evangelical clergy in the NCC orbit who mine the intellectual and social as well as evangelistic facets of the heritage have witnessed the withering of conciliar ecumenism because of its ill-advised pluralistic and political priorities. They find no wholly congenial home in the NAE, however, and probe other evangelical fellowships (Reformed, subdenominational, regional, etc.). Restive participants within all these groups are calling for vigorous alternatives, and they are voicing increasingly strident criticism of the evangelical status quo.

The latest in a rather long succession of volumes about the conservative religious scene is *The Evangelicals*, edited by David F. Wells and John

D. Woodbridge (Abingdon, 1975). Its diversity of contributors—some evangelical and some non-evangelical—leaves unclear just what authentic evangelical Christianity is. Who is speaking definitively? Paul Holmer or Martin Marty or John Gerstner or Kenneth Kantzer?

A great deal has evidently happened since *The Uneasy Conscience of Modern Fundamentalism* (Eerdmans, 1947) when, despite growing conviction that the evangelicals needed to mend some of their ways, there was little doubt as to who they are.

The evangelical high noon of a half-generation ago was not in fact without significant historical antecedents, however much liberal church historians tend to minimize them. To assess the crumbling of evangelical unity we shall need to consider emphases by certain evangelicals earlier in this century and by some in the present. Having burst his cage in a time of theological default, the lion of evangelicalism now seems unsure which road to take.

# 2.
# *Heritage from the Past*

THE FLOURISHING EVANGELICAL RENAISSANCE a half-generation ago was not a creation *ex nihilo*.

Evangelical colleges and Bible institutes were carrying forward a Christian educational heritage forfeited by campuses like Andover, Harvard, and Yale. (Some liberal historians so ignored the founding of their own institutions by evangelical donors that they depicted evangelicalism as a deviant cult.) Still relatively unknown at the

[25]

height of evangelistic crusades by Charles E. Fuller, Jr., Bob Jones, Sr., Paul Rood, John R. Rice, and others like Merv Rosell who came somewhat later, Billy Graham emerged with Torrey Johnson and Bob Cook in massive Youth for Christ rallies. These leaders usually evangelized independently of the tightening ecumenical orbit. Both Charles E. Fuller's "Old Fashioned Revival Hour" and Walter A. Maier's "Lutheran Hour" were attracting immense radio followings long before Graham's "Hour of Decision." With the onslaught of such thriving evangelical programing, the Federal Council of Churches that had preempted most of the available public service opportunities sought federal legislation to prohibit network sale of time for religious broadcasting.

Nor did Fuller Theological Seminary arise out of the blue. Founded with educational trust funds left by the late evangelist's father, it was intended by Fuller to do on the West Coast much of what Westminster was already doing on the East Coast. *Christianity Today*, too, was preceded by magazines like *The Sunday School Times*, *Moody Monthly*, *Christian Herald*, *Eternity*, and *Christian Life*, which on a quite different level sought to link evangelicals across denominational lines. In the mid-thirties, moreover, then President J. Oliver Buswell, Jr., envisaged Wheaton College becoming an academically respectable university that would stress even as did Calvin College the importance of Christian world-life view.

The evangelical resurgence of the last twenty-five years has stimulated ongoing assessment and counterassessment. The hard right has repeatedly sought to tag a renascent evangelicalism with a nonfundamentalist neoevangelical label; for all that, it has failed to curb the reassertion of neglected dynamisms that once belonged to the evangelical heritage. Dominated by debatable criteria, nonevangelical interpreters also strained to demean the evangelical enterprise (cf. Stewart G. Cole, *The History of Fundamentalism*, Richard R. Smith, 1931; Norman F. Furniss, *The Fundamentalist Controversy: 1918–1931*, Yale

University Press, 1954). Some critics sought to pass off evangelical vitalities as a post–World War II phenomenon (Willard M. Sperry, *Religion in America*, Macmillan, 1948; William G. McLoughlin, *Modern Revivalism: Charles Grandison Finney to Billy Graham*, Ronald Press, 1959); others as an excrescence of the Graham personality cult (Ernest R. Sandeen, *The Roots of Fundamentalism: British and American Millenarianism 1800–1930*, University of Chicago Press, 1970, p. ix).

In the ecumenical appraisals of evangelical concerns, biblical and Reformation antecedents were minimized and evangelical continuity in the nineteenth and twentieth centuries was also largely ignored (cf. Winthrop S. Hudson, *Religion in America*, Scribner's, 1965) despite Kenneth Scott Latourette's comprehensive overviews. Some interpreters more accurately brought into focus only the far right (John H. Redekop, *The American Far Right: A Case Study of Billy James Hargis*, Eerdmans, 1968; Erling Jorstad, *The Politics of*

*Doomsday: Fundamentalists of the Far Right*, Abingdon, 1970). Despite mainly liberal-ecumenical sympathies, the two-volume survey by H. Shelton Smith, Robert T. Handy and Lefferts A. Loetscher, *American Christianity: An Historical Interpretation with Representative Documents* (Scribner's, 1960, 1963), reflects evangelical continuities more faithfully than most recent sources because its interpretation is correlated with documentation.

Meanwhile evangelicals themselves engaged in navel-gazing. What were the implications, they asked, of dispensationalism or of long-range Reformation emphases for evangelical renascence?

Edward John Carnell set *The Case for Orthodox Christianity* (Westminster, 1959) over against liberalism and neoorthodoxy, but in doing so alienated dispensational conservatives; almost simultaneously Mennonite scholar C. Norman Kraus depicted dispensationalism as an evangelical deviation (*Dispensationalism in America*, John Knox Press, 1958). Resurgent evangelical

[29]

emphases were scorched in turn by dispensational fundamentalist Robert Lightner (*Neo-evangelicalism*, Dunham Publishing Co., n.d.), while Charles Ryrie also, but with more finesse, differentiated dispensationalism from broader evangelical emphases (*Dispensationalism Today*, Moody Press, 1965).

Still broader issues underlay the emerging fundamentalist-evangelical tensions, however. Louis Gasper's *The Fundamentalist Movement* (Mouton, 1963) saw evangelicals as fundamentalists in high gear, whereas Ronald H. Nash in *The New Evangelicalism* (Zondervan, 1963) and Millard Erickson in *The New Evangelical Theology* (Revell, 1968) wrote from different perspectives.

What distressed the growing evangelical mainstream about the fundamentalist far right were its personal legalisms, suspicion of advanced education, disdain for biblical criticism per se, polemical orientation of theological discussion, judgmental attitudes toward those in ecumenically related

denominations, and an uncritical political conservatism often defined as "Christian anticom-
munism" and "Christian capitalism" that, while
politicizing the gospel on the right, deplored politicizing it on the left.

To protest such emphases and to elaborate pre-
ferred alternatives evangelicals reached behind
twentieth-century fundamentalism and appealed
to a longer past. This longer look encouraged a revolt against pietism not simply disinterested in
but even disdainful of serious intellectual pursuits.
Even more, it gave new urgency to the question
of the implications of the gospel for the socio-
cultural scene from which fundamentalism had
withdrawn. And the longer look raised additional
questions about the stance of evangelicals yester-
day and today in respect to scriptural inerrancy
and authority.

Meanwhile those whose theological emphasis
had long since moved in a different orbit found
the term *evangelical* more and more attractive.
When addressing the American scene, European

theologians labeled their comprehensive theological writings "evangelical," their considerable departure from historic Christian commitments notwithstanding. Notable examples are Karl Barth in his *Evangelical Theology* (Holt, Rinehart and Winston, 1963) and Helmut Thielicke in *The Evangelical Faith* (Eerdmans, 1974).

# 3.
# *Decade of Gains and Losses*

DESPITE A SLOWDOWN IN INITIATIVE AND A crumbling of unity in the last ten years, American evangelicalism has nonetheless witnessed some noteworthy positive developments.

World Vision as an international humanitarian agency has gained remarkable favor as an outlet for the growing commitment to social effort combined with Christian witness; it now has the largest budget of any evangelical enterprise in the world.

Evangelically oriented seminaries (among them Dallas, Denver, Fuller, Gordon-Conwell, Trinity and Westminster) continue to show record enrollments. Meanwhile a growing number of nonevangelical seminaries, their larger financial incentives to students notwithstanding, are in trouble. Inter-Varsity Christian Fellowship has come through its financial slump and has significantly expanded its publications program; its triennial missionary conferences remain vigorous. Campus Crusade continues to enlarge its collegiate evangelistic ministry. The Institute for Advanced Christian Studies has provided over $100,000 to underwrite meritorious research by mature evangelical scholars whose publication fulfillment is high. An impressive complement of competent young evangelicals have completed doctoral studies in prestigious universities. Of these a growing number are teaching on secular campuses and are working on serious academic projects that reflect important Christian concerns.

Evangelical scholars continue to work on Bible translation (the New American Standard Version has been followed by the New International Version) and *The Living Bible* paraphrase (18 million copies have been printed) has gained reader interest in many circles where more traditional versions seemed linguistically remote. Wycliffe Bible Translators continues to extend the availability of Scripture in developing countries.

Dean M. Kelly has correctly observed that, despite the secular cultural pressures on American churches, significant growth is taking place, particularly in the evangelical wing of Protestantism (*Why Conservative Churches Are Growing*, Harper & Row, 1972). Graham Crusades, while fewer and somewhat shorter than in earlier years and in some places under some attendance pressure, nonetheless still provide a focus for cooperative evangelism wherever they occur. A staggering number of youth ministries, counseling, and church renewal programs has added depth to local evangelistic follow-up. The church growth interest nurtured by Fuller Institute of Church Growth gave rise to related books and symposiums (Donald McGavran, *Understanding Church Growth*, Eerdmans, 1969; McGavran, ed., *The Eye of the Storm: The Great Debate in Mission*, Word Books, 1972; Alan R. Tippett, ed., *God, Man and Church Growth*, Eerdmans, 1973). While somewhat decreased in number since the Key '73 boost, thousands of neighborhood house groups still meet regularly for Bible study and prayer.

The emergence of a literature that criticized the evangelical stance and was written by evangelicals themselves proved to be no unmitigated liability. Occasional conservative books on social ethics appearing in the mid-sixties (e.g., David Moberg, *Inasmuch: Christian Social Responsibility in the Twentieth Century*, Eerdmans, 1965, and my own *Aspects of Christian Social Ethics*, Eerdmans, 1964) touched off a veritable tide of literature in the field. Sherwood Wirt's *The*

*Social Conscience of the Evangelicals* (Harper & Row, 1968) and a score of other works appeared in quick succession. Younger church historians like James A. Hedstrom have assessed the appearance in the late sixties "of very honest and critical analysis of evangelicalism itself, by evangelicals" as a constructively significant sign. Hedstrom notes the call for change, for renewal and reform, that issued from the Black evangelical movement (Tom Skinner, *Words of Revolution*, Zondervan, 1970, and *How Black Is the Gospel?*, Lippincott, 1970); and the protest of evangelical historians against cultural conformity (Richard V. Pierard, *Protest and Politics: Christianity and Contemporary Affairs*, Attic Press, 1968; Mark Hatfield, *Conflict and Conscience*, Word Books, 1971; Carl F. H. Henry, *A Plea for Evangelical Demonstration*, Baker, 1971; David O. Moberg, *The Great Reversal: Evangelism versus Social Concern*, Lippincott, 1972). The growing interest in ethics was crowned finally by the cooperative evangelical effort *Baker's Dictionary of*

*Christian Ethics* (Baker, 1973). It led also to the forging by young evangelicals of a notable declaration of social concerns (cf. Ronald J. Sider, ed., *The Chicago Declaration*, Creation House, 1974). Meanwhile, unprecedented numbers of young evangelical students ventured into social service, law, political science, and other public fields as a Christian vocation.

The call for evangelical renewal precipitated and reflected significant divergences. Nothing was more needed at the beginning of the seventies than incisive evangelical theological perspective and influential direction to maintain unity in the midst of creative debate. Francis Schaeffer's L'Abri Fellowship in Switzerland reenlisted some runaway evangelicals for apologetic thrust on neglected cultural frontiers. But divergences multiplied as comprehensive evangelical leadership was increasingly absent. At critical points—especially in the debate over scriptural authority and sociopolitical stance—the movement's institutional spokesmen seemed to lack incisive power. Pronouncements increasingly took the course of reactionary criticism rather than definitive direction.

Billy Graham was the one voice that, in concert with *Christianity Today*, could until five years ago have sparked a massive realignment of American evangelicals in a new and larger fellowship embracing the NAE, many clergy and laymen in ecumenically oriented denominations, and even some loosely committed to the fundamentalist right. But such a move would have aroused denominational resistance to cooperative crusades. Graham's late father-in-law, L. Nelson Bell, had notably opposed an evangelical realignment by Southern Presbyterians. The North American Presbyterian and Reformed Council is currently emerging as a framework to include the Christian Reformed Church, Orthodox Presbyterian Church, Reformed Presbyterian Church (Evangelical Synod), Reformed Presbyterian Church of North America, and the Presbyterian Church in America which separated from the

Presbyterian Church in the U.S. (Southern). The time seems now to have passed in America for the emergence of a comprehensive evangelical paraecumenical movement, if indeed that should have been a desirable development. The charismatic movement, welcomed or tolerated as a potentially potent force for uniting evangelicals across denominational barriers, is now increasingly strained by internal dispute over church authority, tradition and mission, and by external denominational opposition and theological criticism. Southern Baptists have declared charismatic congregations to be divisive.

Meanwhile *Christianity Today* essayists have been drawn more largely from independent sources than from ecumenically oriented denominations. The fortnightly seems also to be putting more and more distance between itself and the call to reexamine the evangelical socio-political stance while tightening a commitment to biblical inerrancy as the determinant of evangelical authenticity.

[40]

# 4.
## Signs of Evangelical Disunity

Notwithstanding the evidence of ongoing vitality, the evangelical movement shows disturbing signs of dissipating its energies and of forfeiting its initiative.

Large denominations once unequivocally aligned with the evangelical enterprise are no longer taken for granted. The Presbyterian Church in the U.S. has already been split into several groups. The Lutheran Church-Missouri

Synod is in a current struggle in which erstwhile ecumenists who once regarded schism as the worst of sins have helped split Concordia Seminary on the issue of biblical criticism. While it retains an evangelical program and evangelistic emphasis, the Southern Baptist Convention in several of its seminaries espouses a murky neoorthodox theology; some of its colleges, no longer unapologetically Christian, even hire faculty members who make no profession of faith whatever. The American Baptist Churches, once thought to be 85 percent evangelical, have faced a steady erosion of conservative strength, American Baptist Seminary of the West in California being the most recent casualty.

Evangelicalism has shown itself painfully weak in shaping American national conscience, despite the massive impact of the Graham crusades and the personal popularity of the evangelist. In the Watergate debacle, a graduate of a leading evangelical college escaped heavier penalties by plea-bargaining and a Baptist was among those imprisoned for illegalities. The shameful national crime statistics, ready acceptance of abortion on demand, serious deterioration of sexual morality, and growing disregard for monogamous marriage indicate how ineffective evangelical proclamation today seems to be in molding the moral sensitivities of the man in the street and sometimes even in the churches and colleges.

While American evangelicals are sometimes estimated to number between 42 and 45 million, individual church statistics are probably inflated by as much as 10 percent through a breakdown in keeping membership rolls current. This dereliction does not alter the overall predominance of evangelicals over nonevangelicals; it does suggest, however, that in proportion to total population, evangelicals may be numerically smaller than sometimes thought. No careful survey has been made of attendance at Sunday evening and midweek prayer meetings, services which tend to survive only in evangelical churches; church school and youth group attendance is notably down, and Sunday evening meetings compete against pressures of the media and transportation and crime problems.

A number of new spiritual forces in American life display little awareness of the church's body-life or else challenge prevalent conceptions of it; many Jesus people, neighborhood study groups, and charismatic gatherings project the same mood of evangelical independency characteristic of their churches, and thus dilute the community impact of a larger fellowship of believers. While the Jesus movement by and large has gained some theological orientation through the Graham crusades and Campus Crusade, and some followers reach for deeper theological roots, others have been drawn into nontrinitarian cults like The Way. The Jesus people as a whole, though remaining an active evangelistic force, are encountering difficulty in enrolling in some Bible colleges because of reputed laxity in serious study.

The evangelical churches in America lack a cohesive integrating structure, leader, or publication that swiftly and cooperatively coordinates their energies. In this respect they differ little from many pluralistically minded churches whose ecumenical canopy has been falling apart. Sooner or later some new pluralistic entity will doubtless emerge. But evangelicals have forfeited their recent opportunity for any major breakthrough on their own. They will likely see younger evangelicals participating increasingly on ecumenical faculties and in ecumenical ecclesiastical alternatives. This situation will invite further disruption from the far right and predictable losses to the left if, as remains likely, ecumenical enterprises are controlled by nonevangelicals who trade power for theological tolerance. Many young evangelical scholars want a larger vision of the church and find little alternative between an objectionable fundamentalist independency and an objectionable ecumenical pluralism. Of the two, they prefer ecumenical tolerance of contradictory views over evangelical intolerance and uncritical acceptance of inherited traditions.

During the past decade, mounting internal tension has beset the American evangelical scene. Persistent criticism has come especially from two groups, those who have switched to a somewhat more critical view of Scripture and those who deplore evangelicalism's seeming cultural captivity and lack of socio-political engagement. Both emphases have in the recent past been shared by influential evangelicals whose positive contributions to the conservative cause earlier in this century are well known to young intellectuals abreast of modern church history.

Sometimes the scriptural and the social concerns overlap, although no logical connection exists between asserting scriptural errancy and supporting neglected scriptural emphases. Those involved in the Scripture debate and in the social debate include Daniel E. Stevick (*Beyond Fundamentalism*, John Knox Press, 1964), Donald Bloesch (*The Evangelical Renaissance*, Eerdmans, 1973), Bernard Ramm (*The Evangelical Heritage*, Word, 1973), and Richard Quebedeaux (*The Young Evangelicals*, Harper & Row,

1974). These scholars voice many legitimate concerns—Bloesch and Ramm in a more mature and balanced way—although their allowances for biblical errancy or myth sometimes elicit diatribes against neoevangelicals and eclipse their proper demand for evangelical reform in other matters.

More and more doctoral students now graduate from nonevangelical institutions that deplore biblical inerrancy as uncritical. They are attracted to the disparate evangelical emphases retained by neoorthodox scholars and cheered by neoorthodox spokesmen who, like John Mackay, have wearied of ecumenical pluralism and commend evangelical dynamisms. Not a few are pressing for bolder evangelical involvement in serious intellectual, cultural, and political engagement; their pleas unfortunately are too often met obliquely or not even heard at all by some who consider inerrancy the only basis on which to speak evangelically on anything. Not a few of these seeking scholars have invested their critical learning constructively in order to advance other evangelically crucial commitments.

# 5.
# *Conflict over*
# *Biblical Inerrancy*

THE ISSUE OF BIBLICAL INERRANCY IS TODAY dividing evangelicals into ever more rigidly competitive camps. The inerrancy emphasis of theologians like Charles Hodge and of New Testament scholars like B. B. Warfield has in the main characterized conservative Christianity in America, and most evangelical colleges, Bible institutes, and seminaries reflect it in their doctrinal commitments. In Britain, where critical theory took a larger toll, emphasis on biblical inerrancy did not as conspicuously dominate the evangelical scene, although the issue has always arisen in evangelical controversy over the authority of Scripture.

The Wenham (Gordon) Conference on Scripture (1966) was a kind of turning point in the inerrancy controversy. Because of inadequate advance planning, the gathering failed to face issues that ought to have been resolved and therefore achieved little more than the predictable conclusion that reputable evangelical scholars are ranged on both sides of the debate. The invasion of neo-orthodoxy into Southern Baptist seminaries eroded emphasis on scriptural inerrancy. Other evangelical campuses, Asbury and Fuller among them, experienced internal faculty disagreement. As Fuller hedged on its original commitment concerning Scripture, the enthusiasm of such faculty members as Wilbur M. Smith, Gleason L. Archer, and Harold Lindsell waned; E. J. Carnell also resisted alteration. In 1961 the Christian Reformed Church was impelled to issue synodical study reports and decisions on biblical infallibility and in 1971 and 1972 on scriptural authority. A major issue in the rupture of Concordia Seminary (Lutheran Church–Missouri Synod) was the legitimacy or illegitimacy of historical critical method in Bible interpretation. Right now the Evangelical Theological Society is in the midst of an unpublicized struggle over its inerrancy statement that some member scholars sign but no longer share.

More and more books and articles support scriptural errancy: e.g., Dewey Beegle's *The Inspiration of Scripture* (Westminster, 1963) and *Scripture, Tradition and Infallibility* (Eerdmans, 1973); Jack Rogers's *Confessions of a Conservative Evangelical* (Westminster, 1974); cf. Richard J. Coleman, "Biblical Inerrancy: Are We Going Anywhere?," *Theology Today*, (January 1975).

Scores of young evangelicals emphasize that scholars uncommitted to inerrancy are producing substantial evangelical works. They repudiate the

[50]

"domino theory" that a rejection of inerrancy involves giving up "one evangelical doctrine after another." They point to the vigorous contributions to evangelical theology by scholars like James Orr in an earlier generation and G. C. Berkouwer, George Ladd, Bruce Metzger, and others in our time; F. F. Bruce, while apparently noncommittal, has written an appreciative introduction to Beegle's last book. Many young scholars invest their own critical learning in defense of evangelically crucial commitments. Some aspire to posts on nonevangelical faculties, aware that an inerrancy commitment seemingly barred the door to competent evangelical scholars in the recent past. Most would be shocked to learn that, for all his concessions to critical theory, James Orr's refusal to go further disqualified him as a scholar in the sight of a former principal of New College, Edinburgh, who disapproved the writing of a doctoral dissertation on Orr's evangelical contribution.

The point is not that biblical inerrancy today

lacks stalwart champions in the succession of J. Gresham Machen, E. J. Young and Ned Stonehouse. Among those champions one might name Geoffrey Bromiley, Gordon H. Clark, Frank E. Gaebelein, Kenneth Kantzer, Roger Nicole, Robert Preus, Francis Schaeffer, Cornelius Van Til, and virtually the entire membership of the Evangelical Theological Society. The view is supported in Clark Pinnock's *Biblical Revelation* (Moody Press, 1972) and John W. Montgomery's *God's Inerrant Word: An International Symposium on the Trustworthiness of Scripture* (Bethany Fellowship, 1974) which includes an essay by the English scholar James I. Packer, even as earlier support can be found in *Revelation and the Bible*, Carl F. H. Henry, ed. (Baker, 1959).

Yet a growing vanguard of young graduates of evangelical colleges who hold doctorates from nonevangelical divinity centers now questions or disowns inerrancy, and the doctrine is held less consistently by evangelical faculties. Some of its supporters increasingly project inerrancy as the hallmark of evangelical fidelity, so that conflict over the issue more and more ruptures the comprehensive unity of evangelical scholars once evident a quarter century ago amid secondary disagreement on this issue.

The present editor of *Christianity Today*, Harold Lindsell, details in *Battle for the Bible* (Zondervan, 1976) the growing rebellion against inerrancy on evangelical campuses. Some retain the term and reassure supportive constituencies but nonetheless stretch the term's meaning. *Christianity Today* has itself come to make inerrancy the badge of evangelical authenticity. Francis Schaeffer projects it as the watershed of evangelical fidelity and deplores a "false evangelicalism" that minimizes inerrancy.

For all their commitment to inerrancy, scholarly evangelicals earlier in this century—Hodge and Warfield included—avoided wholly resting Christian theism upon it. With New Testament balance, their doctrine of Scripture emphasized first of all the divine authority and then the inspiration of Scripture, much as did the apostles. While scholars disagreed as to whether inerrancy is explicitly or only implicitly taught in Scripture, they did not make inerrancy a theological weapon with which to drive those evangelicals not adhering to the doctrine into a nonevangelical camp.

From the very first, *Christianity Today* was editorially committed to inerrancy. But its contributors were drawn from the broad evangelical spectrum to wage literary battle against nonevangelical perspectives. To divide this array of contributors polemically over the issue of inerrancy was not in purview. This does not mean that a reasoned presentation of the epistemological significance of inerrancy is unimportant. The magazine editorially affirmed what is the case, that inerrancy and not errancy is the logical implication of the divine authority and inspiration of Scripture; that champions of errancy have adduced no objective biblical, theological or philosophical criterion to distinguish supposedly errant from inerrant passages; that errancy introduces epistemic instability as evidenced by disagreements over biblical reliability even among its evangelical advocates, let alone among liberal advocates whose irreconcilable differences drove neoorthodoxy to affirm that no part of the Bible is in itself God's Word.

The claim by young evangelicals that to reject inerrancy does not automatically drive one to repudiate other evangelical doctrines is wholly right. The real question is whether, once scriptural errancy is affirmed, a consistent evangelical faith is maintained thereafter only by an act of will rather than by persuasive epistemological credentials. A volitional faith may also affirm that God can and does use poor grammar and may equally use errant statements and resort therefore to a theology of paradox. Paul K. Jewett (*Man As Male and Female*, Eerdmans, 1975) and G. C. Berkouwer (*Holy Scripture*, Eerdmans, 1975) seem to compromise not only the inerrancy but also the normativity of Scripture by differentiating within it a time-bound and a non-time-bound authority.

Yet the appeal to useful contributions made by mediating scholars, and distaste for the use of inerrancy as a polemical weapon in the absence of reasoned supports, must not be ignored. Neither can the increasing fragmentation of evangelical cohesion over the issue of inerrancy. Evangelical churches and campuses that incorporate inerrancy in their statements have every obligation to preserve doctrinal fidelity. But the duty of the evangelical enterprise requires something higher than invalidating every contribution of evangelicals who halt short of that commitment. Those in leadership posts must exhibit the doctrine's rational roots and openly display its intellectual fruits.

# 6.
# *Strife over Social Concerns*

DESPITE RENEWED AWARENESS THAT THE Christian gospel has indispensable social implications, evangelicals seem to divide increasingly over the relation between social concern and evangelism and over what program Christian social ethics implies.

At the far right are fundamentalists who consider evangelism the church's only proper task in the world and justify social effort—like rescue missions and relief for the poor—only as a means of converting others to personal faith. Evangelist Billy Graham is not so extreme; while he distinguishes evangelism as the primary mission of the church, he also recognizes the propriety of an evangelical response to human need generally, and the BGEA has only recently established a framework for evangelical social response. The National Association of Evangelicals, which links a vast network of theologically conservative churches, has more fully channeled the gospel dynamic to such human needs as postwar relief in Europe and South Korea and by means of its World Relief Commission has ministered even more widely through socio-spiritual programs administered by evangelicals in disaster and poverty-stricken areas.

The demand of third-world evangelicals that the Christian gospel not be attenuated to personal conversion but incorporate also a vigorous demand for social justice that indicts oppressive politico-economic forces has shaken up the World Evangelical Fellowship whose American supporters concentrate on personal regeneration. Leighton Ford, John Stott, Bishop Jack Dain and many WEF participants view the restriction to personal conversion as a limitation of the gospel.

A number of evangelical agencies are responding creatively to diverse human needs. Among them are Food for the Hungry, which maintains an evangelical witness and administration in various programs in many countries; Medical Assistance Program, which provides personnel, training, medicine, and supplies in the area of health needs; and the Institute for International Development, which brings together Christian entrepreneurs in fifteen countries and their American counterparts to sponsor job-creating efforts. Giant of them all is World Vision International, a global humanitarian work whose annual contributions by Christians mainly in the United States, Canada, Germany, Australia, and New Zealand now make it the largest existing evangelical agency.

[59]

The cultural conformity of establishment evangelicalism distressed many earnest university students who lived through the racial and the Watergate crises and who began to enunciate socio-ethical imperatives. The Jesus movement, moreover, called for a life-style that lifted believers above the prevalent secular love of money. Criticism of secular capitalism, of racial inequities, and of mounting military budgets in an era of widespread poverty issued in the founding of magazines such as *The Other Side*, *Post-American* (now *Sojourners*), and *Wittenberg Door*. Some spokesmen showed evident sympathy for democratic socialism, as does a vocal vanguard of Latin American missionaries, and several approve certain forms of violence to achieve social change.

Meeting over Thanksgiving 1973, a coalition of evangelicals concerned for social change issued the Chicago Declaration which, with a vigor uncharacteristic of the evangelical establishment, indicts injustices in the American scene. They emphasized that evangelicals and others have social duties to each other, irrespective of religious beliefs, and that promotion of social justice devolves upon everyone. Their annual workshop has now become deliberately diversified both racially and sexually. The vanguard's cohesion is increasingly threatened, however, and its future seems unsure. While the young activists hold divergent views of Scripture, they share the verities of the early Christian creeds and insist on personal regeneration. But like the Jesus movement, they are plagued by evangelical independency and lack a sense of larger Christian community. Participants tend to be committed programmatically rather than to a comprehensive life-world view; they push for support of their own special interests in disregard of impressive minority dissent, show a proclivity to a legalistic imposition of goals where possible, and on the whole harbor exaggerated expectations of the socio-political arena. The loose cooperative character of this thrust has most recently been further strained by the intemperate charges of William Bentley, president of the National Black Evangelical Association. Ignoring anti-racist efforts already represented in the alliance, he accuses the Chicago connection of racism in mood, structure, method, and theology. Inasmuch as the 1975 workshop lost focus on any long-term function and reached no consensus on an undergirding theological statement and model for social action, let alone on any united program, some observers sense the beginning of the end.

This development was painful for some coalition leaders who cultivate closer relations with conciliar ecumenists to shape a common cooperative socio-economic thrust. Renewed evangelical commitment to social engagement has been somewhat fogged by ecumenical depiction of this phenomenon as a belated endorsement of the "social gospel" that a generation ago provoked the fundamentalist withdrawal from ecumenical socio-cultural commitments. But the "social gospelers," in contrast to socially concerned evangelicals, dispensed with the need for personal conversion,

STRIFE OVER SOCIAL CONCERNS

promoted socialism (and sometimes communism) as a divine alternative to capitalism, and considered legislation the instrument for orchestrating the Kingdom of God.

Mennonite spokesman John Yoder declined to sign the Chicago Declaration because he favors (*The Politics of Jesus*, Eerdmans, 1972, and earlier works) larger priorities for the cultural distinctiveness of the Christian community as the new society, including pacificism. Some young evangelicals, on the other hand, emphasize that, for all its faults, the American system is not irremedially wicked and that evangelical initiative can reform it. Paul Henry, political science professor at Calvin College and chairman of the Kent County (Grand Rapids) Republican party, in his *Politics for Evangelicals* (Judson Press, 1974) pleads for Christian political involvement. Like some other young scholars, he overindicts his own heritage by depicting evangelical political indifference as symptomatic of a gnostic denial of the immediacy and reality of the Kingdom in this world. He tends to treat political engagement, moreover, as a test of orthodoxy and views acceptable political engagement somewhat in terms of liberal conservatism. Stephen Monsma, former Calvin professor recently elected a Democratic representative in the Michigan House, in *The Unraveling of America* (Inter-Varsity Press, 1974) also deplores evangelical neglect of political instrumentalities; as a Reformed scholar, however, he is less acerbic about his tradition and he is somewhat a conservative liberal. Young academicians such as these are shaping evangelical student enthusiasm for practical political engagement. Closer to the top in the Washington arena, this activity is exemplified, among others, by Senator Mark Hatfield (*Between a Rock and a Hard Place*, Word Books, 1976) and Congressman John B. Anderson (*Vision and Betrayal in America*, Word Books, 1975).

# 7.
# *Reaction and Realignment*

ONE OF THE CHINKS IN THE ARMOR OF THE contemporary evangelical movement is the defensive and reactionary stance of some of its influential leaders. That was not Billy Graham's perspective in world evangelism nor was it the founding orientation of *Christianity Today*.

What will be the result if the evangelical mainline, like the newly aggressive far right, echoes a religious jingoism that merely ignores or rebukes multiplying nuclei of discontent and forfeits their creative potential? It is not unlikely that neoevangelical forces will pursue theologically mediating and then ecumenically concessive relationships and align themselves with a chastened neoorthodoxy rather than a retrogressive orthodoxy.

Had late nineteenth-century evangelicals more dynamically asserted a truly biblical ecumenism and adequate socio-political interests, had they given exemplary guidance to the forces of discontent and been less resigned to a reactionary withdrawal from newly emerging centers of power, the early twentieth-century churches might have followed a sounder ecumenical and socio-political course. Now the critical question before establishment evangelicalism is whether in the late twentieth century it will duplicate the mistakes of a previous era.

Discernible changes in the evangelical arena are already in the making. Evangelism is seen increasingly as the proper burden of the local church or churches and as best effected through the faithful witness of believers at work and at play. New methodologies are already in wide use, many having been shared through Key '73.

Magazines like *Eternity*, *Reformed Journal*, and *Christian Herald* are openly discussing, even if at times with a debatable emphasis, neglected socio-political concerns, as well as the doctrine of the church and biblical authority, but in a way that candidly wrestles contemporary disagreements. The somewhat reactionary elevation of inerrancy as the superbadge of evangelical orthodoxy deploys energies to this controversy that evangelicals might better apply to producing comprehensive theological and philosophical works so desperately needed in a time of national and civilizational crisis. It is important to know, of course, whether a launch missile can be relied upon unerringly or whether it may malfunction unpredictably; it will never reach the moon, however, if all energies are exhausted in prelaunch debate. The sad fact is that when evangelicals do not engage *en force* in challenging alien world-life views they soon fall into battling among themselves. Things are even sadder when leaders among them set the pattern for such squandering of vitalities. Already mortgaged to the hilt, some evangelical schools threaten to divide on the inerrancy issue; still others are suffering constituency blues at a time when overarching cooperative evangelical effort might have tellingly confronted the radical secularity of our times.

Unless evangelicals repair their multiplying frictions over social and political engagement in an intelligently spiritual meeting of mind and heart, the situation can only result in still further divisions that forfeit whatever impact might have issued otherwise through strategic cooperation. To be sure, political engagement is no more the hallmark of evangelical orthodoxy than is political disengagement. But evangelicals should be publicly concerned to the limits of their competence and ability; here too "to him that knoweth to do good and doeth it not, to him it is sin" (James 4:17).

A restrictive social vision can have only doleful consequences for evangelical conscience and national life. In his resurrection Jesus Christ already displays his sure victory over all the forces of evil and injustice that would have done him to death. If the Risen Lord wishes to extend that victory over unrighteousness in the world through the regenerate community, dare we derail social justice as a marginal concern until he returns as King of all worlds finally to conquer evil and vindicate righteousness? Are only a few evangelical visionaries to champion social justice while supposedly more sanctified saints preoccupy themselves with personal evangelism alone? If God is now the God of justification but has gone into hiding as the God of justice, are we not merely dispensing evangelistic Watergate pardons to people who have no sense of public guilt?

Even if they are motivated by a legitimate defense of capitalism and of democratic processes against socialist and totalitarian assaults, the failure of establishment evangelicals to criticize incisively the American politico-cultural context, including secular capitalism and seamy governmental trends, has often dampened the enthusiasm of the younger generation for these structural forms. Uncritical commendation of the status quo stimulated hypercritical denunciation of it by the political left. Stirred by socialist criticism of capitalism and of Western political processes, American students were left to learn about the real character of Marxism from Solzhenitsyn and Sakharov, who have endured it firsthand. Observable failures of socialism in Eastern Europe, Great Britain and other lands were simply explained away by concentrating criticism on Western alternatives. It is almost forgotten today that an emphasis on the desirable limits of government does not—as advocates of collectivist dogma and social engineering would have it—inevitably commit political conservatives to an atomistic society of windowless monads.

The growing impasse between evangelical groups, each of which deliberately and perhaps stubbornly advances its own approach and emphasis, creates misunderstanding and sacrifices gains that might accrue to the whole evangelical front by solidifying agreements. Such concentration need not ignore legitimate differences. New centers of evangelical power and conviction will almost inevitably come into being in the next decade; what is unsure is whether their input into the total evangelical context will be disruptive or constructive.

At present no single leader or agency holds the full enthusiasm and respect of every element within contemporary American evangelicalism. It may already be too late to gather for dialogue because of explicit rivalries or political liaison between the various groups. While pointing at the disintegration of COCU, evangelicals should remember that their own movement seems brighter not because of evangelical cohesion but because of comparison with the tarnished alternatives which, in fact, are likely to reemerge sooner or later in some other novel form.

Evangelicals today have campus resources far greater than those available and experienced in generations previous to the modernist takeover of various institutions. The newly projected $6 million Billy Graham Center at Wheaton will, for example, greatly enhance the missionary influence of that school. But what evangelicals need most amid the present tide of irrationalism and cultural decay is to enlist all the movement's rational and moral energies for a comprehensive confrontation of the religious, philosophical, and social arenas. By sharing in such a vision, the somewhat lame and halt evangelical forces in all enterprises— from Southern Baptist and Missouri Synod quarters, from ecumenical conciliar quarters, from evangelical establishment sources, from the more radical social activist groups, from among isolated independent spirits who labor with a sense of messianic individualism—could together forge fresh conviction and brilliant truth for redeemed society to proffer a despairing world.

[72]

# 8.
## Toward a
## Brighter Day

NOT ALL PROPOSALS FOR ADVANCE NECESSARILY
guarantee or even promise dramatic evangelical
breakthrough; some may, however, be helpful in
arresting fragmentation and in promoting a de-
gree of progress.

*1.* The basic evangelical need is not for structural reorganization of a paraconciliar sort, nor
for a channeling of evangelical bodies into pres-
ently existing conciliar structures. The future

of the ecumenical cause lies neither in least-common-denominator cooperation nor in ecumenical pluralism, both of which fix attention on sheer numbers and aggregate weight. What evangelical renewal does require is recovery of the larger sense of evangelical family in which fellow-believers recognize their common answerability to God in his scripturally given Word and their responsibility for and to each other within the body of faith. Unless the new society gains visibility as an identifiable fellowship of holy love, righteousness, and joy, Christians will speak to the chaotic fragmentation of national life only in terms of an isolated individual faith that needlessly forfeits the corporate vitalities of the regenerate community. In short, evangelical Christians must repent of the radical independency that aligns believers against believers in a spirit of competition and even of suspicion and judgment. In this context it would be interesting to trace the origin of such pejorative terms as "evangelical establishment," "neos," "fundys" or whatever else—terms which recall the Pauline censure of those who insisted "I am Paul's man," or "I am for Apollos"; "I follow Cephas," or "I am Christ's." "Surely," the Apostle exclaimed, "Christ has not been divided among you!" (1 Cor. 1:12 f., NEB).

What does it mean in the present circumstances of an increasingly divided evangelicalism to invite the world to a fellowship quickened by the Risen Lord and indwelt by the Holy Spirit? The most promising steps in a new direction may best be ventured not in national or regional conventions but in local fellowships where (even if they must first meet in homes to overcome ecclesiastical prejudices or structural animosities) neighbors and townspeople affirm their oneness in Christ as those whose lives are scripturally controlled by the Spirit.

Much of American Christianity is moving into a postdenominational, contraconciliar and non-institutional era. Multitudes are reaching above all else for Christ's headship over the Church, for dynamic renewal by the Spirit, for the light of the authoritative Scriptures on their problems, and for an extended spiritual family that demonstrates and is distinguished for New Testament vitalities within a notably godless society. The cohesive shelter of spiritual unity becomes the more urgent as previous alternatives become increasingly dysfunctional. That is not to say that structural concerns are unimportant. Institutions are indispensable to any movement's durability, and it is a mark of maturity when evangelicals realize that institutions must be properly nurtured and cultivated and their goals persistently deepened. But evangelicals who, in the realm of secular social concern, have long emphasized that significant renewal will not come about by simply altering social structures without personal change, need now to apply this conviction to their own growing disunity.

2. Presentation of a rationale for Christian faith is an evangelical imperative. While it is true that the evangelical movement is conspicu-

TOWARD A BRIGHTER DAY

ously evangelistic, many disenchanted liberal and even neoorthodox observers think conservative Christianity is growing not because its positions are intellectually tenable but rather because of its emphasis on an intimate personal relationship with God, prayer, and inner devotional experience. The anti-intellectualism and intellectual vagrancy of recent modern theology cannot be effectively confronted by overlooking intellectual problems and pressing hurriedly for decision. To be sure, the call for prompt evangelistic commitment commendably enlists many whose lives are emotionally frayed and volitionally frustrated. But it often turns off those who argue that a leap into intellectual darkness exerts no more claim to be authentically Christian than to be subjectively mystical; others it leaves vulnerable to doctrinal counterclaims.

Neither piety nor moralism alone can hope to prevail over the current ethical decline of our day, nor will a blurred presentation of beliefs seriously challenge today's radical secularism and existential subjectivity. Instead of feeling threatened by secular concepts with which they cannot agree, evangelical Christians need to raise up a rationally competent generation that is both literate in the humanities and articulate in its beliefs. Interest in serious theological literature has so deteriorated that some classic landmark books sold two generations ago would now hold little publications appeal. Many evangelicals today are riding the crest of apocalyptic, charismatic, and personal-confession fads. Sales of religious books as such have zoomed in this decade of shifting beliefs and values; on the average, one in every four American families buys at least one religious book every year. The Bible continues to outsell all other religious works, but apart from that, reader interest centers not in theological study but rather in personal-experience—oriented material.

Theological superficiality in congregations often reflects theological leanness in the pulpit. Some ministerial counselors have noted that clergy in continuing education classes frequently opt for case-study courses that presumably help cope with conflict situations with church leaders. Meantime, congregations long for theological preaching that illumines the church members' life-problems. The high diversification of short-interest literature among both Catholics and non-evangelicals discourages secular religious publishers from serious commitments; in some cases religion departments are being absorbed into the general publications program.

In evangelical circles, however, serious religious reading continues to maintain a notable foothold, and the number of laymen who seek a literate faith is on the rise. Zondervan, Baker, and Word have joined Eerdmans in scheduling scholarly works of intellectual merit, and new marketing techniques are confirming the suspicion that a substantial and appreciative market exists for theologically significant publications. The most influential theological scholarship will doubtless continue to be that of devoted individuals who earnestly grapple with the problems of the day. Enduring systematic theology is not done by symposium or team effort, however valuable such joint ventures continue to be.

The present crisis in theology—a period in which the most influential ecumenical scholars disagree over the very nature and task of the discipline—calls qualified evangelicals to invest their fullest energies to produce serious theological, philosophical, and biblical literature in the entire spectrum of theological controversy and engagement. To expedite this task, evangelicals might well inventory international resources that include both extant literature and qualified academics. By defining areas of need and enlisting competent scholars to grapple with them both independently and cooperatively, the many fields of inquiry could be competently covered.

# 9.
# *Moving on*
# *Media Frontiers*

*3.* WE EVANGELICALS MUST INSPIRE THE MASS media to picture-window evangelical realities to the restive world. Satellite radio and television may soon overtake the field; frontier studies are now underway to determine the possibilities of launching a Christian satellite or of leasing time on already orbiting satellites. Television, America's prime communications medium, far surpasses the earlier popularity of the theater, newspapers, and radio; 98 percent of the people now watch it, many of them almost addictively. Vigorous media engagement is all the more necessary if, as Malcolm Muggeridge contends, television promotes cultural decline by implicitly, if not explicitly, commending moral permissiveness as the virtue of modernity. No less does the medium accommodate cultural chaos by routinely evading the issue of fixed truth. Like the United Nations, television is far more a forum for spirited presentation of conflicting opinions than a tribunal for promoting discernment of right and wrong.

If evangelicals had launched a major university that included a college of creative and communicative arts to train Christian young people for vocations in writing and editing, radio and television, stage and screen, the Christian message would today enjoy wider and better audibility and visibility in the media arts. Evangelical programing still falls largely into the so-called "Sunday ghetto." No evangelical agency has as yet

[82]

developed a regular prime-time weekday program that effectively and directly confronts secular society with the Christian challenge. For one thing, the cost of such programing is staggering; beyond that, inter-network competition for assured audience ratings discourages the sale of prime time for religious purposes. The consecutive jumble of intensely powerful programs swiftly erodes and actually precludes establishing any firm emotional and volitional impact and viewer response. Much better follow-up analysis should be made of media postal respondents.

The Lansman-Milam petition to thwart the designating of educational FM and TV channels for religious organizations has been disallowed by the Federal Communications Commission. The objection that sectarian stations do not program contrary views was a veritable Pandora's box: it would alternately conform every station to a complainant's point of view and surface implications of "fairness" for secular stations dealing all too sparingly with the evangelical heritage,

[83]

although evangelicals are now appearing at least occasionally on television talk shows. More than 700,000 letters deluged the FCC with an evangelical appeal for a nondiscriminatory ruling. The FCC expects all licensed stations to observe the "fairness" doctrine, and it stresses the need for constructive community relationships both in program policy and in implementing professional standards, truthfulness, effective techniques, and relevant content.

A number of independent Christian radio networks and television stations are already functioning at the borders of large, wildly secular urban centers. Some evangelicals see cable television programing as an alternative to station ownership and operation. Recently, charismatically oriented groups have moved aggressively into media frontiers. Oral Roberts has sporadically invaded prime-time television with a mixture of musical entertainment and spiritual ministry; meantime, Pat Robertson's fifty-four radio and television outlets engage in direct evangelistic confronta tion, as do more traditional programs like replays of major Billy Graham crusades. The fortnightly *National Courier*, targeted for bookstore and shopping center sale, is the latest of various charismatic efforts.

Most evangelical television programs, if not sermonic in nature, are largely experience- and event-oriented. World Vision has successfully sponsored famine-appeal telethons and televised other evangelical social concerns. For the most part, Christian theism, if presented at all, is done in an intellectually unpersuasive way to a generation in revolt against doctrinal and theological foundations for biblical faith. While evangelical programing does not on that account lack merit, it nonetheless fails to reflect comprehensively and cohesively the biblical view of life and the ultimately real world at a time when the great urban centers with their universities, newspapers, and other media have largely capitulated to secular pressures.

Enough evangelical churches are in sufficient

financial or attendance trouble to warrant consideration of using at least one strategically located inner-city church building for high-quality FM or educational TV religious programing. Such a center might also offer Christians possibilities of training in writing, music, art, photography, and so on. The growing use of cassettes in extending educational preaching and evangelistic ministries is notably enlarging the perspectives of clergy, seminarians, and laymen. Their fullest potential remains to be probed.

Wherever they are, evangelical college students should be counseled to pursue elective classes in journalism and creative writing. While the content of writing is in the long run most important, a felicitous style does much to commend the truth in winsome ways and can gain a hearing when ideas run counter to popular prejudices. The temptation to capitulate to the devil is stronger when deception is cloaked in sparkling speech; why should not the truth be all the more regally robed? In this realm C. S. Lewis has put the devil to rout and the rest of us to shame.

4. Evangelical churchmen will do well to re-evaluate existing Sunday programs as to nature, serviceability, and timing. While local worship ought not to be reshaped by a particular media mentality, it need not be or remain drab. Sunday morning programs that involve the family in both graded and corporate participation in worship, education, and social fellowship offer challenging possibilities. To avoid the overall proliferation of church meetings, decline in youth involvement, and erosion of the church school, and to solve the isolation problem of lonely members are high imperatives. No longer will just any prescribed headquarters format meet the varied needs of varied congregations. With an eye on the immediate church families and community context, local leaders can examine existing needs; by enlisting, wherever possible, resources within the church they will not only meet those needs

[87]

specifically but will also promote leadership training. In some places Sunday evening church meetings might preferably be given over to high school and college age groups while older adults gather in neighborhood Bible studies or engage in prayer and testimony meetings or conduct seekers' or new converts' classes. Three-day weekends, four-day work weeks, crises in safety, transportation, and so on call for imaginative scheduling and programing. A proper balance of worship, evangelism, Christian education (including arts, crafts, and writing as potential evangelical tools in communication), service projects, and recreation can do much to demonstrate the wholeness of the gospel for the whole person for the whole world.

# 10.
# *Vision of*
# *a Uniting Task*

MANY EVANGELICALS, LONGING FOR SPIRITUAL
normalcy in the best sense of the word, are quite
ready to supersede obsolete institutional loyalties
and to follow more challenging life-charts. Desir-
ing the evangelical community to be what it ought
to be, they are ready to venture upon more biblical
ways. They will not, however, be bludgeoned and
persuaded into new paths. They are waiting for
trusted leaders who will rally fragmented forces

to comprehend and implement the new vision of a uniting task.

Too often, unfortunately, these leaders champion their own special causes as the superhighway into the future. Many discerning laymen know, however, that a numb conscience is one of Satan's choice wishes for the evangelical community and too easily reconciles Christians to the unmet needs of the age. Not a few of the clergy, particularly younger ministers, know this as well. To rely merely on already existing resources and on frontier techniques perpetuates evangelical deficiencies and postpones their solution.

Fortunately, for all its tensions, the evangelical movement is not deeply haunted by the pluralism that embraces radically contradictory beliefs. Evangelicalism insists and relies, moreover, on the regenerating reality of the Holy Spirit to enliven spiritually those who find forgiveness of sins through the crucified and risen Lord. And it demonstrates much of the moral power that distinguishes a redeemed people from and within

[90]

their secular milieu. In our sexually adolescent and aberrational age, evangelicalism fosters wholesome family resources. In a time when, for multitudes, work lacks meaning and challenge, it can define vocation in terms of divine calling and human service. In a land of greying goals and values it can stress anew the nation's answerability to God who gave it birth and preserves it still for justice at home and abroad. Evangelicals have abundant vitality which, if properly realized and applied, can energize both them and the world with promise and hope.

Yet we often deport ourselves in the public scene like outcasts to Russia or China; we resign ourselves to a subculture, if not underground existence. That is the surest way for a minority—and Christians are likely to be a minority in many, if not most, places—to turn the possibility or threat of mere underground survival into actuality. Our churches are more frequently cities of refuge than launch-pads to invade a secular society that in the past has made the Puritan distasteful and is trying in the present to make the evangelical no less so.

We need first and foremost a fresh touch of fire upon our lives and lips. There is little to fear from this age of anti-intellectualism. Ecumenists have become "manythingarians"; Unitarians are phasing into "nothingarians" and liberals are fading into "anything-and-everything-arians." Trinitarians have seldom had so opportune a day in which to champion the claims of revelational theism: it is nothing short of high tragedy to withhold or curtail a bold evangelical witness. Perhaps we have too many alien alliances to present evangelical Christianity forthrightly and persuasively; perhaps we have substituted clichés for conscientious conviction and need to reinstall informed dedication. Perhaps television routinely robs too much time better given to serious reading and contemplation, not to mention prayer and Bible reading. Perhaps our love of God has paled and we need, in keeping with our own message, to return in contrition to the Risen Lord who asks, "Lovest thou Me?"

Some key evangelicals are not even on speaking terms, let alone on learning terms with each other. How does one speak convincingly to the world of a body whose members are indispensable to each other when the arm disowns the head or the mouth declares of the ear, "I have no need of you"? How do erstwhile Christian co-workers drift apart? How do charismatics invalidate each other's tongues and even go to court with each other while trumpeting charisma as the deepest unifier of the Christian community?

Perhaps we ought to listen in on what our children are saying—those who resist part of what was their evangelical heritage because they desire greater loyalty to Christ and the Word. It would be illuminating to have a major evangelical dialogue that involved not simply elder statesmen but younger statesmen as well, like John Woodbridge, Clyde Donald Taylor, Thomas McIntire,

Richard Kantzer, Marlin VanElderen, John Walvoord, Tom Howard, Stephen Monsma, Don Wyrtzen, Paul Henry. We might learn whether in overcoming the polarities of the recent past they are simply rearranging these polarities, whether they are enmeshed in new polarities of the emerging future, or whether they are blessed, as we hope, with insights that assure a better day.

Those who declare that unabashed commitment to biblical inerrancy guarantees theological vitality have the past twenty-five years of meager production by the Evangelical Theological Society to explain. Those who contend that personal evangelism best guarantees national sensitivity to morality and social justice have the breakdown of public ethics to explain. Those who maintain that doctrinal consensus best guarantees ecclesiastical unity have to explain the ongoing divisions among evangelicals whose churches have much more in common theologically than do ecumenical congregations. Those who insist that God frowns upon any and all cooperation with those outside

[94]

our own ecclesiastical structures should honestly examine the fruits of such exclusivity. Those who contend that the theology of revelation is the most persuasive context for forging world-life concerns must explain the dearth of serious philosophical exposition of rational theism in our evangelical college circles. At a time of civilizational crisis evangelicals either need to rethink some of their assumptions or need earnestly to repent of faith deficient in works.

In modern warfare, supremacy at sea means little without supremacy in the air; in Christian engagement, evangelistic success and social change devoid of theological truth and power are but temporary and vulnerable gains. Social change without evangelistic regeneracy easily capitulates to radical excesses or unexpected reversion; theological profundity without evangelistic compassion spawns arid ecclesiastical introversion. We are fighting in the modern world with seriously impaired strength if we think that even at the human level the evangelical cause

[95]

depends mainly on the evangelist or the theologian or the social activist per se, and does not involve a three-pronged phalanx that gives each his due.

While we supposed leaders champion our special interests and assure our followers that the evangelical prospect was never brighter because of what we represent, more and more discerning Christians are asking what has happened to comprehensive, coordinated leadership that stimulates not only evangelical initiative but also evangelical reconciliation. It is time that the evangelical movement sees itself for what it is: a lion on the loose that no one today seriously fears. The crafty beast stalking us at every turn is Satan, who, lionlike (1 Pet. 5:8), would undo us and our cause; only in the shelter of the Lion of the tribe of Judah (Rev. 5:5) can we prevail.